LIFE IN THE
FREEZER

LIFE IN THE
FREEZER

with a specially-written text for young people

ALASTAIR FOTHERGILL

With photographs by
BEN OSBORNE

Introduced by
DAVID ATTENBOROUGH

BBC CHiLDRENS BOOKS

PICTURE CREDITS

BBC Children's Books would like to thank the following for providing photographs
and for permission to reproduce copyright material.

All photographs are by **Ben Osborne** except: **Doug Allan** pages 22 and 62;
Ardea (Auscape/Mike Osmond) page 26; **Alastair Fothergill** pages 64 and 69;
Planet Earth Pictures (Peter Scoones) page 27(bottom);
Graham Robertson pages 8–9, 11, 60–61, 66(bottom) and 67;
Stephen de Vere page 66(top)

Published by BBC Children's Books,
a division of BBC Enterprises Limited,
Woodlands, 80 Wood Lane
London W12 0TT

First published in 1994

© Alastair Fothergill 1994
The moral right of the author has been asserted

ISBN 0 563 40378 0

Designed by Judith Robertson

Printed and bound in Great Britain by Butler & Tanner Limited, Frome, Somerset
Colour separations by Radstock Reproductions Limited, Midsomer Norton
Jacket printed by Lawrence Allen Limited, Weston-super-Mare

Front cover: *King penguins during courtship.*
Rear cover: *Crowds of furry brown chicks in a king penguin breeding colony.*
Page 1: *A grey-headed albatross chick sits in its nest, waiting for its parents to return with food.*
Page 2: *A wandering albatross tests the wind before taking off.*
Page 5: *In the king penguin colony.*

Contents

Exploring Antarctica

Standing in a huge colony of macaroni penguins on Bird Island, right at the edge of the Antarctic, it would be difficult to feel lonely. The macaronis are sociable creatures, and here they breed in a vast settlement of around 80,000 pairs. In early summer, the squawking and squabbling noise in the colony is deafening!

Yet much of Antarctica is not like Bird Island at all. There are huge stretches of desolate land, barren ice and empty sea, where even the toughest animals are few and far between. Human visitors are even rarer, and the freezing cold and biting winds make it impossible for anyone to live there without special equipment.

The cold is incredible, particularly on the Antarctic mainland in the far south. Before stepping out of doors, you need to put on layers of warm insulated clothing and, even though Antarctic gear is now made from modern, lightweight material, it is still so bulky that no one can move around quickly in it. Making a series of wildlife programmes in these conditions was especially difficult.

Yet Antarctica is also one of the most beautiful and fascinating of all the world's wild places. Each species of animal that lives there has had to develop its own unique ways of coping with the harsh conditions. The results of their struggle with the elements can be truly amazing. The macaroni penguins are probably some of Antarctica's noisiest and most colourful inhabitants. But they are just one part of the range of plants and animals which go together to make up the rich pattern of life in the freezer.

David Attenborough

The Coldest Place on Earth

Why So Cold?

If you go outside on a hot summer's day and look up at the sky, you'll see that the sun is almost directly above your head. Its warm rays seem to beat straight down onto the Earth. But in winter the sun stays much lower in the sky; even when it is shining brightly and clearly, you can still feel the cold.

In Antarctica, the sun never shines from directly overhead. Even in summer, the sun stays low in the sky and the temperature at the South Pole remains well below freezing point. During the Antarctic winter (from April to October) conditions become even harsher. Then, the South Pole gets no sunlight at all. There are six months of total darkness, and the temperature plummets to −70 °C.

The height of the land and the thick layer of ice on top of it add to the intense cold at the South Pole. Antarctica is a huge landmass, higher than any other continent on the Earth. The average height of the land is 2,300 m. With every 100 m that you climb above sea level, the temperature drops by 1 degree centigrade. Even when the sea is already frozen solid around the coastline, it is always another 20 °C colder at the centre of the Antarctic continent.

▷ *Because of the way that the Earth tilts to one side in relation to the sun, Antarctica never receives direct, overhead sunlight. The only bird to survive on the Antarctic mainland during the long, dark winter is the emperor penguin.*

▷ *The islands of the Southern Ocean around Antarctica are some of the stormiest on Earth. The wandering albatross chicks that are born there have to sit through their first winter blizzards when they are just a few months old.*

Just like Antarctica, the Arctic region around the North Pole suffers from the lack of overhead sun, but never becomes anything like as cold. There is no land at the North Pole, and although the sea freezes solid in winter, the warming influence of the water beneath means that the ice is never more than a few metres thick.

Surviving the Cold

Compared with any other place on Earth, Antarctica is home to a very small number of different species of plants and animals. Yet all the creatures that live in the far south have one thing in common: each has developed its own special and ingenious ways of surviving in the cold. In fact, some species are so successful that they have huge populations, flourishing in conditions that are too harsh for other kinds of animal.

There are no land mammals at all on mainland Antarctica. Not even the king of Arctic wildlife, the polar bear, exists in the numbing conditions of winter in Antarctica. Those animals that do live in the Antarctic survive there because they are cleverly adapted to life in and around the sea. Amongst these animals are mammals, such as whales and seals, and many birds, including penguins, petrels and albatrosses. Nearly all of these creatures take their food from the sea – and when winter fixes the Antarctic mainland in its icy grip, all except the emperor penguins escape to the warmer conditions of the Southern Ocean and its islands.

▽ Penguins cannot fly, and on dry land they waddle around clumsily. But they are expert divers and swimmers, perfectly equipped for hunting in the Southern Ocean.

△ Apart from humans, there are probably more crabeater seals than any other large mammal on Earth. They never come to dry land, but spend their whole lives at sea, with ice floes as resting places.

▷ The wandering albatross is the world's largest sea bird. It flies huge distances by gliding along on air currents. This is the ideal way to travel across the stormy seas of the Southern Ocean where there is never a shortage of wind.

The Lonely Continent

Where does the Antarctic begin? Strictly speaking, it is anywhere below the Antarctic Circle, the latitude line at 66° 32' south. At this point, there is at least one day of total darkness at midwinter. However, most scientists and sailors think of the Antarctic as anywhere south of the Antarctic Polar Front. This is the line where cold water from Antarctica meets warm water flowing south from the tropics. The exact position of the Polar Front changes from year to year but it is always between 50° and 60° south.

South of the Polar Front is the Southern Ocean, the stormiest, windiest seas on Earth, with winds that can blow at a record 300 km per hour. Set in the northern part of the Ocean are a few tiny sub-Antarctic islands, which are home to much of the region's wildlife. In summer, these islands are the greenest part of the continent, and even in winter they are never cut off from the ocean by sea ice.

▽ *Most of Antarctica is covered by a huge sheet of ice, which in some places is over 4,000 m thick. It started to form 30 million years ago and today it holds about 90 per cent of all the world's fresh water. Only the mountain tops are tall enough to stand out above this vast layer of ice.*

The Antarctic Continent

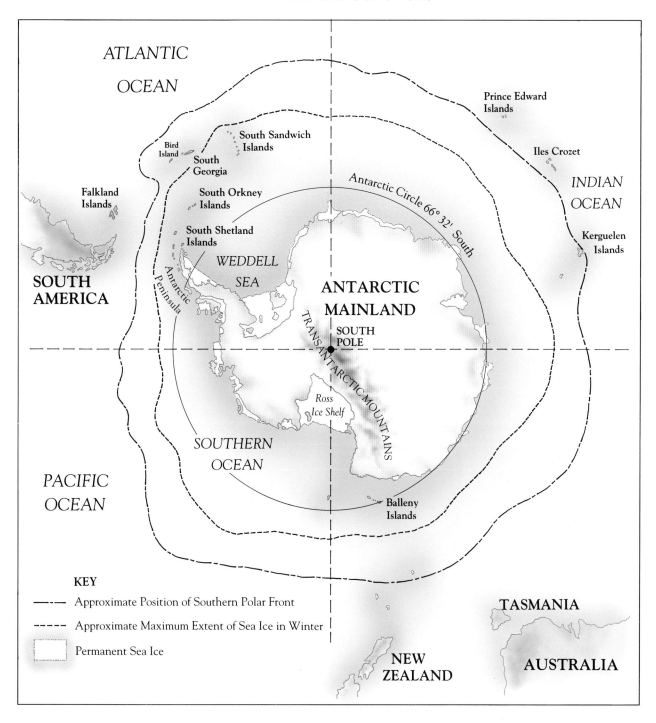

Further south again are several chains of small, rocky islands – the maritime islands – and Antarctica itself, which is also called the Antarctic mainland. Bigger than the USA and Mexico put together, this is the most isolated landmass on Earth. Its distance from other continents across the barrier of the wide open ocean helps to keep Antarctica the coldest and loneliest place on Earth.

The Ice Machine

Every winter, the deep land ice of mainland Antarctica is enlarged by another kind of ice – sea ice. In the biggest single environmental change on Earth, a huge area of the Southern Ocean freezes over. As the weather grows colder, about 20 million square kilometres of sea turn to ice and the Antarctic mainland is cut off from the open sea. The frozen sea closes Antarctica off from the rest of the world. No ship, not even a large, modern icebreaker, can make its way through.

The sea ice begins its advance each autumn. At first, ice crystals form, and, as these crystals squash together, they turn into a thick layer of ice. As the weather grows even colder, the sea ice expands more quickly, until it can grow in area by 100,000 square kilometres each day. By the end of the winter in September, the sea ice covers up to 57 per cent of the whole Southern Ocean. It does not begin to break up again until the spring is underway. Then, at last, the ice slowly retreats towards the Antarctic mainland once more.

▷ *When the solid sea ice melts in spring, it starts by breaking down into a jigsaw of smaller pieces called pack ice.*

A glacier at the edge of mainland Antarctica. Most of the sunlight which reaches Antarctica is reflected back off into space by the huge amount of ice; the continent only actually absorbs heat from the sun during November and December.

The Bountiful Sea

In the choppy seas of the Southern Ocean this elegant, striped iceberg towers above the 15 metre-tall mast of a passing yacht.

The Southern Ocean

The Southern Ocean has the roughest weather conditions of any sea on Earth. Powerful winds race around the globe and huge seas build up, with no land to get in the way of the enormous waves and break them up. Anyone venturing into the ocean sets out on a dangerous voyage. In good weather, the shortest crossing to the Antarctic Peninsula from the Falkland Islands takes just three days. In bad weather it can take weeks.

Another hazard for sailors in the Southern Ocean are icebergs. As a ship crosses the Polar Front, it begins to meet these great floating lumps of ice. The smallest, called growlers, are about the size of a car, but the largest can be as big as cathedrals. They come in all shapes, eroded by the action of the sun and the sea, and they vary in colour from electric blue to dazzling white.

Ships keep a constant look-out for approaching icebergs, and radar now helps sailors to spot them, but they still pose a threat to travellers in the Southern Ocean. Even a huge, modern icebreaker may be damaged and sink if it collides with a very large iceberg.

◁ It is easy to forget that something as beautiful as an iceberg can also be deadly. This berg could crush any small boat that ran into its path.

The Food Chain

All the animals that live in Antarctica are linked together in a food chain: small creatures are eaten by larger ones, which in turn are food for even bigger animals. In Antarctica, this chain is made possible by a single vital element – the ocean.

The smallest links in the Antarctic food chain are not animals at all, but tiny plants called phytoplankton. They live near the surface of the water, making food for themselves from sunlight during the summer. They also feed off the nutrients, or minerals, that are especially plentiful in the Southern Ocean.

The phytoplankton are themselves eaten by tiny sea creatures or zooplankton. These are in turn eaten by small, pink shrimp-like animals called krill. Krill are about 5 cm long and live in thick swarms. Stretching for kilometres, these swarms turn the sea a strange pink colour. They are the staple food of many Antarctic creatures, from whales and seals to penguins and other birds.

▽ *The Antarctic food chain connects many different living things in one great ecosystem. This leopard seal has just captured a penguin chick. Penguins themselves eat krill and other sea creatures, which in turn feed on smaller animals and phytoplankton.*

▷ Fur seals are also important hunters of krill. The seals regularly swim distances of 60–90 km from shore looking for swarms.

◁ Scientists estimate that there are 600 million krill in the ocean, which makes them by far the most numerous sea creature on Earth.

◁ An Antarctic tern returns to its nest with freshly-caught krill. Humans also fish for krill, but, luckily for Antarctic wildlife, we do not like it very much. Once krill has been caught, it tends to go rotten very quickly.

◁ A South Georgia pintail duck eating the flesh of a dead fur seal. Ducks are not usually meat-eating birds and the pintail cannot rip skin with its own beak. But once a larger bird has made a hole in a carcass, the duck will put its head right inside.

▽ Skuas are powerful, aggressive birds. Each pair marks out its own territory with a long, ear-splitting call, which warns off other birds.

Scavengers

Hunting is not the only way of finding food. Some animals in the Antarctic – particularly birds – also feed off the scraps of flesh abandoned by other creatures. These are the scavengers.

Sheathbills are the Antarctic's refuse collectors. About the size of crows, they are the only birds which do not hunt for seafood at all, but live almost entirely off what other animals have left behind. Penguin droppings are an important part of their diet, and they pick at any dead flesh they can find. They also snatch food out of the mouths of penguins who are about to feed their chicks.

▽ This dead elephant seal provides food for scavenging giant petrels. Birds belonging to a smaller species of petrel, the cape petrel, wait to gather the scraps.

If sheathbills are the refuse collectors, giant petrels are the vultures of Antarctica. They fish for krill, but add to this food by scavenging any dead flesh they can find and preying on penguin chicks. Skuas are even fiercer. Sometimes they attack smaller birds in flight, forcing their victims to give up any food they have caught for their young. Skuas are also partial to penguin eggs. To steal these eggs they work in pairs; one bird will pull a penguin off its nest by its tail, while the partner makes off with the egg.

Whales

At the very top of the Antarctic food chain are the whales, the undisputed rulers of the Southern Ocean. Over 10 different species swim south each summer to feed in the rich waters, but they can be split into two clear groups: baleen whales and toothed whales.

Baleen whales include the humpback whale and the blue whale, which grows to 30 m long and is the largest living creature on Earth. In spite of their vast size, these creatures live mainly on krill. On the roof of the whale's mouth are two rows of horny baleen plates, which the whales use to scoop up krill from the sea and then sieve or filter the creatures out of the water.

Toothed whales usually eat a wider variety of food. Some live mainly on squid, but the fiercest species of all, the killer whale, hunts seals and will even attack baleen whales.

▽ *Over the last hundred years, many whale species have become endangered. They have been hunted for their meat and blubber, or fat. Humpback whales were particularly easy to hunt because they tend to stay close to coasts. Now most whales are protected by international law.*

△ A resting humpback whale breathes out a mixture of warm air and moisture. This is the whale's spout.

▷ Humpback whales usually hunt krill in pairs or small groups. They sometimes swim around the krill in a wide circle, blowing bubbles which force the krill closer and closer together into a trap. In this photograph, you can see the whale's baleen plates which sift the krill.

Riders on the Wind

Whales may be the rulers of the Southern Ocean, but the magnificent albatross is the king of the skies. These large, powerful birds are perfectly adapted to live in the blustery conditions of the Antarctic's northern edge, and there are four species that live there. The largest is the wandering albatross, with its huge wing span of around 3.5 m, twice the length of two adult humans lying head to toe. These birds fly at an average 30 kilometres per hour, but can reach a top speed of 88 kilometres per hour.

All albatrosses fly in the same way. The bird begins by making a dive, with its wings held in an 'M' shape, to reduce its resistance to the wind and build up speed. As it gets close to the surface of the sea, the albatross turns along the trough of a wave and straightens up its wings. The air current coming off the crest of the wave then lifts the albatross back up into the air and it quickly regains height. It glides along for a while until it begins to lose speed, when it simply dives and starts the whole cycle again.

▽ *Grey-headed albatrosses form mating pairs that usually last for life. Each summer, the pair returns to the same nesting site. They sit on the nest, preening one another's feathers in what looks like a state of total happiness.*

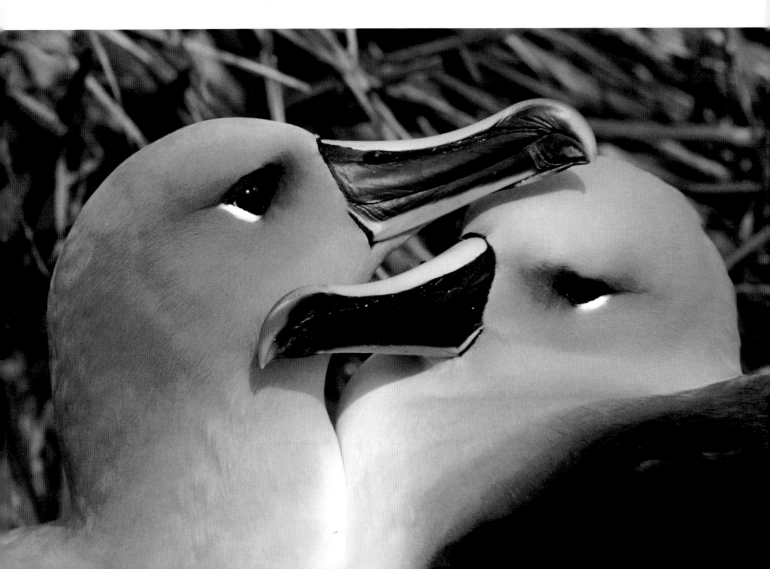

△ *A black-browed albatross catching the wind above one of the islands where it breeds. The birds are also known as mollymawks.*

The albatross flying technique means that the birds can travel for enormous distances for days on end without using up much energy or coming back to land. In fact, the birds spend most of their lives alone at sea, and only really return to the islands on the edge of Antarctica to breed and feed their chicks. However, albatrosses do need lots of wind, and they hardly ever stray far from the blustery conditions between the latitudes of 40° and 50° south.

For many years, scientists could only study albatrosses when they were at their nesting sites, but new technology has helped us to learn more about them. It is now possible to fit a tiny electronic radio transmitter to the back of an albatross and track its movements by satellite as it flies around the Southern Ocean.

Islands on the Edge

The Crowded Colonies

◁ Every year more than 2,500 pairs of wandering albatrosses nest on Bird Island at the northern tip of South Georgia. The albatrosses often live for over 80 years and usually stay with one breeding partner for their entire lives.

On the very edge of the Antarctic, just inside the Polar Front, are a handful of sub-Antarctic islands. They have a milder climate than anywhere further south. In summer the average temperature is around 3 °C, and the weather is often wet and windy. In winter the islands are rarely cut off by the sea ice that traps the mainland. Compared with the rest of the continent, the islands also seem very green, with their tussock grass and several flowering plants.

These islands are vitally important for Antarctic wildlife. For many animals they are the only places to breed. During the summer months seals and many different species of sea bird gather there to raise their young. Some breeding animals make their homes in large, thickly-packed crowds called colonies.

However, some animals also stay on right throughout the winter. The wandering albatross, for instance, is such a large bird that its chick takes over 12 months to grow into an adult, and the young bird spends the first whole year of its life in its nest on one of the sub-Antarctic islands. The albatrosses breed only once every two years, when the female lays just a single white egg.

▽ A male albatross displays to its mate while another female looks on.

Growing up in Winter

The egg laid by the wandering albatross takes about 78 days to incubate. The two parents both take turns at sitting on the nest, each keeping the egg warm for three to ten-day shifts. When it finally hatches, the chick weighs about 350 g. But it grows quickly and within seven weeks it has reached around 3 kg.

At this stage, the parents go off to sea to look for food, and the chick stays behind to sit out the worst of the winter weather. The parents return to feed it once every three days or so, but sometimes they are delayed by storms and the chick is left alone for weeks.

By the spring, the chick has lost its warm protective coat of down, and, as it sits on its nest, is almost as tall as a human. It now starts to practise flapping its wings ready for its first flight. At last it runs towards a cliff and takes off, disappearing into the air.

No one knows exactly where the young albatrosses go, but scientists believe that they spend the next few years flying around Antarctica. After about five years, they return to their home island. They eventually begin to mate a couple of years later.

▽ *Like many other birds, the wandering albatross passes food to its chick by regurgitating. The adults eat the food they catch, but only partly digest it. Later they can bring the partly-digested food back up out of their stomachs and give it to the chick.*

◁ The egg laid by a female wandering albatross weighs almost half a kilogram. If the chick is to hatch, one of the parents must always stay on the nest to keep the egg warm.

▷ During the winter, the wandering albatross chick keeps on building up its own nest until it is sitting on quite a high mound of earth and grass. Even on top of this tall nest, a chick can be completely buried if there is a heavy snowfall!

King Penguins

Like the wandering albatross, king penguins also breed on the sub-Antarctic islands. These dignified, handsome birds reach almost a metre in height. Because it takes from 16 to 18 months for a newly-laid egg to become a fully-grown adult, there are always colonies of young birds on the islands, whatever the time of year.

The penguins have a complicated breeding cycle. Each year, some pairs are first-wave breeders; they mate in early spring and their chicks hatch in early summer. When winter draws in, these chicks are already quite large, and by the following summer the young penguins are fully grown and ready to go out to sea.

Other penguin pairs are second-wave breeders. They were usually first-wave breeders the year before, so they do not lay their eggs until the first-wave chicks have left the colony in midsummer. When winter comes on, the second-wave chicks are still small and many of them do not survive the winter. Those chicks that do survive are not fully grown until autumn in the following year.

▽ *King penguins on the beach at St Andrew's Bay, South Georgia. After taking a bath in the sea, getting back onto dry land is not always easy, and some of the penguins are thrown down onto the beach by the foaming surf.*

▷ As a part of their complicated courtship ritual, king penguins lift their heads high in the air to show off the beautiful yellow-orange patch of feathers on their necks.

King penguin colonies are always on flat ground near the sea. An ideal place is often at the mouth of a melting glacier, on the land that has been worn down by the ice. Some colonies contain hundreds of birds, others are home to thousands. The largest, on the Iles Crozet, has over 300,000 pairs.

In the Penguin Colony

King penguins are unusual birds – they do not build nests. Instead, the adults hold their egg on their feet, underneath a flap of skin that keeps it warm. When the eggs hatch, the penguin chicks do not seem much like their parents at all. They have thick coats of fuzzy brown down, and from a distance look just like small furry bears.

As the winter draws on, the adult birds go to sea to look for food. Now the chicks all stay close together for warmth and protection against other animals. The parents often stay out at sea for four to six weeks and may go as far as 250 km to search for small fish and squid. They are skilled divers and can go as deep as 290 m. Each time the parents return to the colony, they bring home as much food as they possibly can, but during the winter the chicks actually lose weight. The weakest die of cold or hunger.

The chicks do not begin to grow again until the spring, when the food supply increases. Then they are finally ready to shed their brown coats. Once they have grown the new black and white feathers of the adult birds, they set out to sea themselves.

▷ *During the summer, a king penguin colony is a busy place. These fully-grown chicks are almost ready to shed their furry winter coats of brown down, while the adult birds are already starting their courtship displays.*

▽ *King penguins guard their eggs from anyone or anything that gets too close.*

Elephant Seals

During the winter, king penguins have the surf and beaches of the sub-Antarctic islands to themselves, but in early spring they are joined by less elegant animals. Elephant seals are about 5 m long, and weigh up to a hefty 4 tonnes. They get their name from their long snouts which look rather like elephants' trunks.

Almost as soon as the females arrive at the breeding colony, they give birth to new seal pups that they have been carrying since the previous summer. For the next month, the mothers feed their pups with milk, and the young seals gain about 9 kg in weight each day.

▽ *The struggle to mate with a large group of females leads to vicious fighting between the males. Each seal pulls itself up to its full height and makes a threatening roar before attacking its opponent.*

Female elephant seals are ready to mate again within three weeks of giving birth. The male seals are very aggressive and try to mate with as many females as they can. The biggest, strongest males defend as big a group of females as possible. However, the weaker males, over two-thirds of the total, are kept away from the females altogether.

Although elephant seals seem clumsy on land, they are amazing swimmers, and their thick layer of blubber keeps them warm out at sea. Because they are mammals, they have to come up to the surface now and again to breathe, but they spend a huge amount of their lives (up to 90 per cent of the time) underwater. They dive to 1,500 m looking for fish and squid, and their eyes are specially adapted to find food in the murky depths.

The Sun Returns

Spring Arrivals

◁ *During the Antarctic summer, even large icebergs begin to melt. They never disappear quickly however. It can take up to ten years for a large berg to be broken down by the sun and the action of the waves.*

In Antarctica, 21 September is an important date. On this day every year the sun rises at the South Pole for the first time in six months, ending the long, cold stretch of winter darkness.

From now on, the Antarctic will gradually become a little warmer. Spring storms break down the edge of the sea ice and some of the simple plants and animals that live in the Southern Ocean begin to breed. Suddenly, more and more food becomes available for the larger creatures further up the food chain.

As spring goes on, animals who have spent the whole winter out at sea looking for food come back to land to breed. Other creatures, such as humpback whales, return from much further afield. They are attracted by the rich swarms of krill and other sea creatures. The most amazing of the summer visitors is a bird, the Arctic tern. It migrates a staggering 12,000 km from the Arctic, looking for food. In the autumn, it returns to the Arctic to breed. By flying the length of the Earth from pole to pole twice a year, the tern spends over three-quarters of its life in almost continuous daylight.

▽ *Some blue-eyed shags stay at their nesting sites on the outskirts of Antarctica all year round. Others migrate south to the Antarctic Peninsula each spring as the sea ice melts.*

▷ *Every spring, some Antarctic skuas return from as far to the north as California and Britain.*

Fur Seals

By the end of October, spring is well underway. Antarctic fur seals are just one of the species that make for the sub-Antarctic islands to breed, and most of the seals head for one island, South Georgia. Each male, or bull, seal tries to claim a patch of the breeding beach and mate with all the females in that territory.

Fur seals are named after their thick, warm coats. They have an outer layer of stiff, water-resistant hairs, which protects an inner layer of fine insulating fibres. This inner layer contains over 40,000 hairs per square centimetre.

In the nineteenth century, so many seals were killed to make fur coats for humans that the animals nearly became extinct. By the 1930s so few were left that they became almost impossible to catch. Fortunately, however, fur seal populations have increased again in recent years and there are now over one and a half million seals in the Antarctic. Their survival may have been helped because humans have also hunted another animal, the baleen whale. Like the fur seals, these whales are big eaters of krill, and the falling population of whales has left more krill for the seals. As fewer and fewer whales eat less and less krill, there is more food left for the fur seals.

▽ *Fights break out on the fur seal breeding beaches if a newly-arrived bull seal tries to take away territory and females from another bull seal. At first the two males try to frighten each other by lifting themselves up on their flippers with their heads in the air. If neither male backs down, the seals push and bite at each other.*

◁ Almost as soon as they reach the breeding beach, female fur seals give birth to a pup they have been carrying all winter. About a week later, they return to sea to hunt for krill, coming back to the beach regularly to feed the pup. The pups live off their mother's milk for almost four months before they are ready to fish for krill themselves.

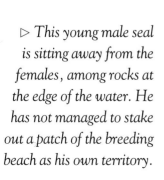

▷ This young male seal is sitting away from the females, among rocks at the edge of the water. He has not managed to stake out a patch of the breeding beach as his own territory.

Petrels

◁ *Snow petrels turn some of the food they eat into a rich oil in their stomachs. This oil seems to be a concentrated energy source which can be carried conveniently over the long distances from the feeding grounds back to the petrels' nests.*

As spring arrives, petrels begin nesting throughout Antarctica. Related to the albatrosses, there are several different species of petrel, each adapted to life in a particular part of the continent.

Burrowing petrels, such as the white-chinned petrel and the blue petrel, build their nests on the sub-Antarctic islands. They make their homes in burrows among the tussock grass, where their chicks will be safe from their enemies. Southern giant petrels, on the other hand, make their nests from loose stones on rocky outcrops of the bleaker, southern islands close to the Antarctic Peninsula.

Snow petrels go even further south. They sometimes nest on the high isolated mountain tops sticking out above the mainland ice sheet itself. For some of these birds, every feeding expedition to the ocean means an amazing round trip of over 360 km.

◁ *White-chinned petrels keep their eggs on a platform of earth and grass in their burrow. That way, even if the burrow is flooded by melting snow, the eggs stay dry.*

▷ *Southern giant petrels are scavengers that also hunt for penguin chicks. They nest close to the penguin colonies on rocky islands such as the South Shetlands.*

Macaroni Penguins

Macaroni penguins make up some of the biggest colonies of spring breeders in Antarctica and there are about 5 million pairs on South Georgia alone. They are quite small birds, each with a tuft of bright yellow feathers on either side of its head. Like the king penguins, they breed on the sub-Antarctic islands – but while king penguins found their colonies on flat beaches, the macaronis are great climbers and nest on steep, rocky slopes.

The male penguins arrive in the colony first and find their nest sites. The macaronis are noisy, aggressive birds and each defends its own patch of ground by pecking and squawking. As a newcomer makes its way through the colony it is quite likely to be attacked by its fellow penguins, and sometimes fights break out.

The macaronis have a mysterious breeding pattern. They lay two eggs – a small one and a large one. However, the first, smaller egg is often destroyed during the squabbles. If it does survive, it hardly ever hatches anyway. Scientists think that possibly the macaronis used to produce two chicks, but are now moving towards always producing just one each year.

▷ *Over hundreds of years macaronis have worn grooves in these rocks that lead to a breeding colony.*

▽ *A macaroni penguin trying to reach its own nest is often attacked by other birds. Sometimes, two birds lock their beaks together in a fight, and both of them end up tumbling down through the colony and into the sea at the bottom!*

Gentoos and Chinstraps

◁ Like other penguins, gentoos do feed on krill, though they also eat small fish which they catch in the shallow waters near to the coast.

▽ Chinstrap penguins lay two eggs each year. In contrast to the two macaroni eggs, there is a good chance that both chinstrap chicks will hatch. Gentoos also produce two good eggs.

Compared with the noisy, quarrelling macaronis, gentoo penguins are much calmer, quieter birds. Some gentoos nest next door to the macaronis on South Georgia, but they also breed on the islands further south. They even form breeding colonies on the Antarctic Peninsula. To reach these southern colonies, the birds have to wait for the sea ice to melt, and in the far south the gentoos do not actually lay their eggs until November.

Chinstrap penguins also breed in the south, on the Antarctic Peninsula and the rocky islands nearby. One large colony is on Deception Island, a volcano which last erupted in 1971. The volcano still has hot springs that melt the snow early, making it a good place for the chinstraps to build their nests.

You can easily tell the chinstrap penguins from the gentoos because the chinstraps are smaller in height and have a clear back band (the 'chinstrap') around their necks. Chinstraps are good climbers too. On Deception Island, they actually nest up near the rim of the volcano, a 90-minute climb from the sea.

Plants and Insects

Apart from at the very edge of the continent, Antarctica is a harsh environment for plants and insects. Besides the intense cold, species living further south must also manage without fresh water – during the winter any moisture is trapped as ice. Yet some plants and insects do exist even on the Antarctic mainland. For most of the year they lie dormant, neither moving nor growing, but in the short summer, they come to life.

The commonest plants are simple lichens. They can live without soil, and survive on exposed rock faces that catch the sun. However, they grow very slowly indeed. Most lichens take a hundred years to spread by just 15 mm.

Life is also hard for insects and other tiny creatures, such as springtails and mites. They live inside mosses and lichen, or even in cracks in the bare rock. If they freeze, these creatures will die, but the very toughest can cope with temperatures below –50 °C because their body fluids contain chemicals that act like antifreeze. Some fleas also survive in Antarctica by living on visiting birds.

▽ *Antarctic hairgrass is one of just two flowering plants that grow on the mainland. It takes root in the tiny amounts of soil made by moss and lichen.*

▷ *In summer, patches of snow are coloured red and green by the simplest plants of all – algae. The algae come to life when a little snow melts and releases fresh water.*

▽ *Over the years, lichens can make just enough of the sandy soil that mosses need to grow. Scientists have discovered about 85 different species of moss on Antarctica and the nearby islands.*

◁ Because they are born so far south, Adélie chicks must grow up quickly and take to the ocean before the sea freezes over again. This chick already has most of its adult feathers, but is probably only about 50 days old.

▽ Adult Adélies live on krill, which they regurgitate to their chicks. On average, Adélie parents feed their chicks once a day.

Adélie Penguins

Adélie penguins are similar to the chinstrap and gentoo penguins, but nest even further south. There are some large colonies on the mainland, and one of them is only 1,300 km from the South Pole itself. All the Adélie breeding sites are on the coast, though the penguins usually arrive before the sea ice has broken up completely and have to walk the last 20–40 km to reach their colony.

Although they are smaller than most other penguins, the Adélies are tough birds. Like many Antarctic animals, they have a thick layer of fat which protects them from the cold and is also an energy store for the long periods when they might go without food. In addition, Adélies have unusual short bills, covered for half of their length in feathers to keep them warm. The birds also keep their nostrils tightly shut to cut down on any loss of body heat.

Like the chinstraps and gentoos, the Adélies lay two eggs, which take about seven weeks to hatch. At first, the chicks must stay close to one of their parents, but once they are about two weeks old, they can wander about on their own.

▽ Going to sea for the first time is a frightening moment for a young Adélie penguin. An adult bird jumps in ahead to show the way. At first, the young Adélies just bob up and down on the surface, but they quickly learn how to dive and make their way through the water.

Preparing for Winter

By early March, the first signs of winter appear; the days grow shorter and the sea ice begins to expand again. Whales, seals and birds all start to move north to warmer waters. Most penguin chicks in the far south have already gone out to open sea, but the adults must stay in their colonies a little longer. Before winter really sets in, they will shed, or moult, their old feathers and grow a new set to keep them warm throughout the coming year.

Growing a new coat uses a great deal of energy, so the penguins begin by feeding furiously to build themselves up. Then they return to their colony and stand, stock still and silent, for up to three weeks while their new feathers gradually replace the old ones.

▷ Compared with the breeding season, a chinstrap penguin colony is a much quieter, stiller place when the birds are moulting. The ground is covered with a carpet of old white feathers that the birds have shed.

▷ A king penguin, half way through moulting. You can see the new feathers on those patches of the bird's body where the old ones have already fallen off. In the harsh conditions of Antarctica, it is essential for the penguins to have a brand new coat of warm feathers every year.

The Big Freeze

Winter on the Ice

Once winter sets in, the Antarctic mainland is a truly deserted place. Apart from a handful of scientists, just one species of penguin, one kind of seal and a few tiny, dormant insects will spend winter there.

Some Weddell seals spend their entire lives in the permanent sea ice on the edge of the mainland. Each animal is equipped with a set of powerful teeth, which it uses to grind away at the ice and keep a breathing hole open all year round. This gap in the ice is essential to the seals' survival – without it, they would be trapped on one side of the ice without food, or on the other side of the ice without air.

Weddell seals are large creatures, reaching up to 3 m in length and 400–500 kg in weight. They spend most of their lives in the water, which is warmer than the temperature above the ice, and they can survive for over an hour without coming up for air. The males defend their breathing holes fiercely, and each male mates with several different females in an underwater breeding territory around its hole.

▽ Weddell seals rarely live to be older than about 20. Constantly grinding away at the ice eventually wears down their strong teeth, and they can no longer keep open the breathing hole they need to survive.

△ Female Weddell seals give birth to their pups in early spring. They feed the pups with their milk, which contains about 60 per cent fat and is richer than that of almost any other animal. The pups go for their first swim in the warmer water below the ice when they are just over one week old.

◁ As winter draws on, the sea ice slowly increases in area once again. Strong winds will suddenly blow together loose pack ice such as this. Boats that are caught in the shifting ice may be crushed and sunk.

Emperors of the Antarctic

◁ Emperor penguins are stately, solid creatures. Although they are not as tall as a fully-grown man, they are often as broad-chested.

▽ In the autumn, when all other animals are heading north, emperor penguins appear at the edge of the sea ice. They leap out of the water and set off for their traditional breeding sites, walking and coasting across the ice on their stomachs.

Emperor penguins are perhaps the toughest of all the animals in Antarctica. They have an astonishing life cycle, and unlike any other bird or mammal actually spend winter on top of the sea ice surrounding the mainland. They survive months of almost total darkness, temperatures that can drop to −60 °C and the fiercest winds and blizzards on the planet.

Emperor penguins look quite similar to king penguins; they stand about one metre tall and have the same white fronts, black wings and orange-yellow neck feathers. However, the emperors have adapted for the extremely harsh conditions of the deep south.

The emperors are much fatter than the king penguins, and weigh 30–40 kg. They have a thick layer of blubber which protects them from the cold and is a store of energy. Their feathers are packed tightly together, and fit over one another to make a coat that is four feathers thick. The birds also have especially small feet and bills, to cut down the amount of body heat that they lose. The veins in their feet and flippers lie close together to keep their blood warm.

◁ Without the protection of an adult's pouch to keep it warm, the emperor penguin egg and young chick would soon freeze to death.

▽ Once they are eight weeks old, the emperor penguin chicks must leave the protection of their parents' pouches and face the worst of the Antarctic winter weather.

Young Emperors

Emperor penguins breed in winter so that the young birds are ready to go to sea in spring when there is most food for them. The female lays an egg in early May, and passes it straight to her mate, who puts it in a pouch just above his feet. She then returns to sea and feeds for the next 65 days. The males are left alone for the next two months to keep the eggs warm in the worst of the winter weather.

The females return to the colony just as the eggs are hatching in the males' pouches. In the darkness the only way for the birds to recognize each other is by the sound of their voices, and the females call to their mates as loudly as they can. When they find one another, the females take over the egg and the males set off across the ice to feed again. After two months without eating, the males look ragged and scrawny, and are desperate for food.

From now on, the males and females take turns at feeding their chick, which by eight weeks is too big for the parents' pouches. In December, both parents return to the sea for good, and the young birds are ready to fend for themselves.

▽ *To keep warm, male emperor penguins huddle together closely in a pack. The group is constantly moving around, so that each bird takes a turn in the coldest positions on the outside of the huddle.*

Footsteps in the Snow

For millions of years, no human laid eyes on Antarctica. The first person to sail south of the Antarctic Circle was Captain James Cook in 1773, but it was another fifty years before anyone saw the mainland itself. No one actually set foot on it until 1895.

Today, about 3,500 scientists work on Antarctica in the summer, and you can even visit the continent as a tourist, travelling by plane or on an icebreaking ship. Sea ice and bad weather still cut off Antarctica from the rest of the world in winter, but the region is more open than ever before to human activity.

Some conservationists would now like to declare the continent a World Wilderness Park to protect it for ever from human development. Whatever happens, we can only hope that all human visitors will treat the Antarctic and its wildlife with care and respect. That way, future generations too will be able to marvel at the wonders of life in the freezer.

▷ *The author at the South Pole. The first explorer to reach the Pole was a Norwegian named Roald Amundsen, in December 1911. He was followed a month later by Robert Scott, whose party died of exposure while returning to their base. Since 1957 there have been a research station and an observatory at the South Pole.*

▷ *Antarctica does not belong to any individual country, but is governed by an international agreement called the Antarctic Treaty. Scientists from any country may work there freely, as long as their research is for peaceful purposes and does no harm to Antarctica's wildlife. Recent scientific studies of birds such as the wandering albatross have increased our knowledge about the ecology of the entire Antarctic region.*

Glossary

Antarctic Circle An imaginary line drawn around the Earth at the latitude of 66° 32' south. Anywhere south of this line has at least one day of total darkness in midwinter.

Antarctic Peninsula The thin strip of land that juts out from the Antarctic mainland towards South America.

Antarctic Polar Front The line all around Antarctica where warm water and air from the north meet cold currents from Antarctica. The seas around the Polar Front have some of the stormiest weather on Earth.

Baleen whale A whale that has baleen plates in its mouth. The whale uses its baleen plates to sieve krill out of the seawater.

Blubber A type of fat. Many Antarctic animals have a layer of blubber beneath their skin to help keep them warm.

Ecology The connections between living creatures and the places where they live.

Glacier A huge sheet or moving river of ice which spreads out across a plain or down the length of a valley.

Iceberg A large block of floating ice.

Incubation After a bird has laid an egg, it must be kept warm until the chick is ready to hatch. Keeping the egg warm is called incubation.

Latitude The latitude of a place is its distance north or south of the Equator, measured in a unit called degrees (°). The Equator has a latitude of 0°. The South Pole, which is the most southerly place on Earth, has a latitude of 90° south.

Mammal Any animal which has warm blood, does not lay eggs and feeds its babies with milk from the mother's own bodies. Most mammals live on land, but whales and seals, which spend their lives at sea, are also mammals.

Moult When an animal grows a new coat of fur or feathers it loses its old coat to make room for the new one growing beneath. Losing the old fur or feathers is called moulting.

Pack ice An area of sea covered in a jigsaw of broken-down pieces of ice. Most pack ice is found between the open sea and the edge of the sea ice, or fast ice.

Phytoplankton Microscopic plants which live in the ocean. They provide food for tiny sea creatures called zooplankton.

Regurgitate When an animal regurgitates, it brings food back up from its stomach. Many birds feed their chicks by first eating food themselves and then regurgitating it for the chicks later.

Scavenger Scavengers, such as skuas or giant petrels, eat up the food that has been killed or left behind by other animals.

Sea bird A bird which takes its food from the sea. Almost all the birds in Antarctica are sea birds which live on fish and krill.

Species A kind or type of plant or animal. Emperors, Adélies and gentoos are all species of penguin, for instance.

Zooplankton Tiny creatures which live in the sea. They provide food for bigger animals such as krill and even whales and sea birds.

Index